The Measure
of Our Success

D0376258

The Measure of Our Success

A Letter to My Children and Yours

Marian Wright Edelman

HARPER **PERENNIAL**

HARPER ● PERENNIAL

A hardcover edition of this book was published in 1992 by Beacon Press. It is here reprinted by arrangement with Beacon Press, 25 Beacon Street, Boston, MA 02108.

HarperCollins books may be purchased for educational, business, or sales promotional use. For information please write: Special Markets Department, HarperCollins Publishers, Inc., 10 East 53rd Street, New York, NY 10022.

First HarperPerennial edition published 1993.

Designed by Aimee Shifman

Library of Congress Cataloging-in-Publication Data
Edelman, Marian Wright.
    The measure of our success : a letter to my children and yours /
Marian Wright Edelman. — 1st HarperPerennial ed.
        p.   cm.
    Originally published: Boston : Beacon Press, c1992.
    ISBN 0-06-097546-6 (paper)   ISBN 978-0-06-097546-3
    1. Child rearing—United States.   2. Children—United States—
Conduct of life.   3. Afro-American children—Conduct of life.
4. United States—Moral conditions.   5. Edelman, Marian Wright.
I. Title.
[HQ769.E355   1993]
649'.1—dc20   92-54846

06 07 08 RRD H 45 44 43 42 41 40 39

This book is dedicated to the legacy of my parents,
Arthur Jerome Wright and Maggie Leola Wright,
and to their children's children:
Joshua, Jonah, and Ezra
Julian Jr., Stan, Stephanie, and Crystal
Debbie, Harryeta, Harry Jr., and Schwannah
Pandit, Arthur Jr., and Krishna
Joy and Maggie

Contents

1. There is no free lunch.
Don't feel entitled to anything
you don't sweat and struggle for.

2. Set goals and work quietly and systematically
toward them.

3. Assign yourself.

4. Never work just for money or for power. They won't
save your soul or help you sleep at night.

5. Don't be afraid of taking risks or of being criticized.

6. Take parenting and family life seriously
and insist that those you work for and who
represent you do.

CONTENTS

Foreword

T HE 8 × 10 PHOTOGRAPH of my parents' wedding occupies a prominent place in both the living room of my house and the recesses of my mind. A record of the pivotal event in the lives of my father and mother, it also signifies my strikingly diverse heritage. In the middle of the nuptial scene stand my parents, with my uncles and aunts, now long since gray, and grandparents, some since gone, at their side. To my father's right, the group are Minneapolis Conservative Jews, three generations removed from Russia, one generation removed from poverty. My grandfather, stern as always, beckons me to persevere as he did. Grandpa supported his entire family from age twelve, when he peddled papers on the freezing corners of St. Paul for nickels and dimes. He exudes the satisfaction of having raised both himself and others up, but grimaces as if to tell me that the fight is far from over. To the left of my mother, the wedding participants are Black Baptists from Bennettsville, South Carolina. They stare fiercely into my eyes, urging me to carry on a tradition forged with sweat, toil, and pride in the cotton field and the pulpit.

My mother, Marian Wright Edelman, has carried on the values of her father and mother, dedicating her life to helping others as a child advocate. Probably one of the most honest people in the world, she is tirelessly devoted to both her children and her cause.

The legacy of our parents and ancestors influences each of us in different ways. Unlike many people my age, I am acutely aware of my family's past. It has for me proven both overwhelming and motivating, burdening and uplifting. I wonder how I would have reacted if I had come up against the obstacles that so many of my relatives struggled to overcome. And I am aware that my mother's is an especially difficult and challenging example to follow, especially in a time in which causes are easy to find but hard to champion effectively, and in which children are earlier and earlier conceived but more and more difficult to nurture.

Our eras as well as our legacies shape us, and in this certainly I am no exception. Born in 1970, I am indebted more than most to the civil rights movement and the struggles of many, like my mother, who exposed and fought racism despite inordinate risks. In fact, I think, had there been no civil rights movement, I would not be the person I am today. My parents might still have met in Mississippi in 1967, gotten married in 1968, and had three children. Josh first, Jonah (me) in the middle, and Ezra last. In the absence of the civil rights period, though, the person that I have become—the cultural mulatto, the well-to-do Black liberal wary of the political process, the sheltered Bar-Mitzvah boy who has struggled with his blackness—never could have existed. Society, I do not believe, would have allowed someone of such a diverse heritage to develop.

My parents raised me to be an individual, letting me make my own mistakes and supporting me when I did. When I spelled m-e-n wrong in the first grade spelling bee (with a capital M as on public bathrooms), they immediately informed me that they were proud of me anyway. Similarly, when I committed three errors in one inning during the biggest varsity baseball game of my young career, they consoled me gently. I did not realize it then, but the phrase, "We are *very* proud of you," always with the emphasis on *very*, boosted me immeasurably through the years. It still does.

Just as I have gained an appreciation for the praise heaped upon me, I also now value the mix of discipline and understanding exhibited by my parents. For instance, my stuffing peas, beans, and other greens in various pockets so as to avoid having to eat them was a minor offense and was dealt with as such by my parents. To them, though, my stealing a candy bar from a store was not a trivial matter. My giving my Dad "the finger" from my shortstop position in Little League for bench-coaching me—in front of every parent in the neighborhood—met with surprising reserve and humor. My coming home in high school at 4:00 A.M. and trying to convince my mother, after frantically stripping off all of my clothes when I heard her calling me, that I had been sleepwalking did not meet with a similar reaction. Though comical, it was blatantly dishonest and resulted in one of the only two groundings I ever received. Through such punishments and my parents' lectures, I was made to learn the importance of honesty and forthrightness. Just as my parents' praise transformed itself into self-confidence, so their lectures became part of me as well.

The publication of my mother's book is a project I have both feared and welcomed—feared because everyone will realize the legacy to which I am tied and the standards I feel responsible to uphold; standards by which few except my mother could live. But I welcome it for the same reason, as it will spur me on. My mother's book is a written testament to her beliefs, from which everyone, including myself, can benefit. Many of her lessons for life strike a chord in me, but three in particular represent what I have come to see as the legacy of my ancestors:

1. Don't feel entitled to anything you don't sweat and struggle for.

2. Never give up. You can make it no matter what comes. Nothing worth having is ever achieved without a struggle.

3. Always remember that you are never alone. You are loved unconditionally. There is nothing you can ever say or do that can take away my or God's love.

When I am feeling paralyzed by a task that seems too difficult, I remember the love that lies at the core of my family and their legacy to me. The love gives strength, and I can move again.

Jonah Martin Edelman
New Haven
November 1991

PART ONE

A Family Legacy

S OUTH CAROLINA is my home state and I am the aunt, granddaughter, daughter, and sister of Baptist ministers. Service was as essential a part of my upbringing as eating and sleeping and going to school. The church was a hub of Black children's social existence, and caring Black adults were buffers against the segregated and hostile outside world that told us we weren't important. But our parents said it wasn't so, our teachers said it wasn't so, and our preachers said it wasn't so. The message of my racially segregated childhood was clear: let no man or woman look down on you, and look down on no man or woman.

We couldn't play in public playgrounds or sit at drugstore lunch counters and order a Coke, so Daddy built a playground and canteen behind the church. In fact, whenever he saw a need, he tried to respond. There were no Black homes for the aged in Bennettsville, so he began one across the street for which he and Mama and we children cooked and served and cleaned. And we children learned that it was our responsibility to take care of elderly family members and neighbors, and that everyone was our neighbor. My mother carried on the home after Daddy died, and my brother Julian has carried it on to this day behind our church since our mother's death in 1984.

Finding another child in my room or a pair of my shoes gone was far from unusual, and twelve foster children followed my sister and me and three brothers as we left home.

Child-rearing and parental work were inseparable. I went everywhere with my parents and was under the watchful eye of members of the congregation and community who were my extended parents. They kept me when my parents went out of town, they reported on and chided me when I strayed from the straight and narrow of community expectations, and they basked in and supported my achievements when I did well. Doing well, they made clear, meant high academic achievement, playing piano in Sunday school or singing or participating in other church activities, being helpful to somebody, displaying good manners (which is nothing more than consideration toward others), and reading. My sister Olive reminded me recently that the only time our father would not give us a chore ("Can't you find something constructive to do?" was his most common refrain) was when we were reading. So we all read a lot! We learned early what our parents and extended community "parents" valued. Children were taught—not by sermonizing, but by personal example—that nothing was too lowly to do. I remember a debate my parents had when I was eight or nine as to whether I was too young to go with my older brother, Harry, to help clean the bed and bedsores of a very sick, poor woman. I went and learned just how much the smallest helping hands and kindness can mean to a person in need.

The ugly external voices of my small-town, segregated childhood (as a very young child I remember standing and hearing former South Carolina Senator James Byrnes railing on the local courthouse lawn about how Black children would never go to school with whites) were tempered by the internal voices of parental and community expectation and pride. My father and I waited anxiously for the *Brown v. Board of Education* decision in 1954. We talked about it and what it would mean for my future and for the future of millions of other Black children. He died the week before *Brown* was decided. But I and other children lucky enough to have caring and courageous parents and other adult role models were able, in later years, to walk through the new and heavy doors that *Brown* slowly and painfully opened—doors that some are trying to close again today.

The adults in our churches and community made children feel valued and important. They took time and paid attention to us. They struggled to find ways to keep us busy. And while life was often hard and resources scarce, we always knew who we were and that the measure of our worth was inside our heads and hearts and not outside in our possessions or on our backs. We were told that the world had a lot of problems; that Black people had an extra lot of problems, but that we were able and obligated to struggle and change them; that being poor was no excuse for not achieving; and that extra intellectual and material gifts brought with them the privilege and responsibility of sharing with others less fortunate. In sum, we learned that service is the rent we pay for living. It is the very purpose of life and not something you do in your spare time. ✳

When my mother died, an old white man in my hometown of Bennettsville asked me what I do. In a flash I realized that in my work at the Children's Defense Fund I do exactly what my parents did—just on a different scale. My brother preached a wonderful sermon at Mama's funeral, but the best tribute was the presence in the back pew of the town drunk, whom an observer said he could not remember coming to church in many years.

The legacies that parents and church and teachers left to my generation of Black children were priceless but not material: a living faith reflected in daily service, the discipline of hard work and stick-to-it-ness, and a capacity to struggle in the face of adversity. Giving up and "burnout" were not part of the language of my elders—you got up every morning and you did what you had to do and you got up every time you fell down and tried as many times as you had to to get it done right. They had grit. They valued family life, family rituals, and tried to be and to expose us to good role models. Role models were of two kinds: those who achieved in the outside world (like Marian Anderson, my namesake) and those who didn't have a whole lot of education or fancy clothes but who taught us by the special grace of their lives the message of Christ and Tolstoy and Gandhi

and Heschel and Dorothy Day and Romero and King
that the Kingdom of God was within—in what you are,
not what you have. I still hope I can be half as good as
Black church and community elders like Miz Lucy
McQueen, Miz Tee Kelly, and Miz Kate Winston, extraordinary women who were kind and patient and loving with children and others and who, when I went to
Spelman College, sent me shoeboxes with chicken and
biscuits and greasy dollar bills.

It never occurred to any Wright child that we were
not going to college or were not expected to share what
we learned and earned with the less fortunate. I was
forty years old before I figured out, thanks to my
brother Harry's superior insight, that my Daddy often
responded to our requests for money by saying he didn't
have any change because he *really* didn't have any rather
than because he had nothing smaller than a twenty dollar bill.

I was fourteen years old the night my Daddy died.
He had holes in his shoes but two children out of college, one in college, another in divinity school, and a
vision he was able to convey to me as he lay dying in an
ambulance that I, a young Black girl, could be and do
anything; that race and gender are shadows; and that
character, self-discipline, determination, attitude, and
service are the substance of life.

I have always believed that I could help change the
world because I have been lucky to have adults around

me who did—in small and large ways. Most were people of simple grace who understood what Walker Percy wrote: You can get all As and still flunk life.

Life was not easy back in the 1940s and 1950s in rural South Carolina for many parents and grandparents. We buried children who died from poverty (and I can't stand it that we still do). Little Johnny Harrington, three houses down from my church parsonage, stepped on and died from a nail because his grandmother had no doctor to advise her, nor the money to pay for health care. (Half of all low-income urban children under two are still not fully immunized against preventable childhood diseases like tetanus and polio and measles.) My classmate, Henry Munnerlyn, broke his neck when he jumped off the bridge into the town creek because only white children were allowed in the public swimming pool. I later heard that the creek where Blacks swam and fished was the hospital sewage outlet. (Today thousands of Black children in our cities and rural areas are losing their lives to cocaine and heroin and alcohol and gang violence because they don't have enough constructive outlets.) The migrant family who collided with a truck on the highway near my home and the ambulance driver who refused to take them to the hospital because they were Black still live in my mind every time I hear about babies who die or are handicapped from birth when they are turned away from hospitals in emergencies or their mothers are turned away in labor because they have no health insurance and cannot pay pre-admission deposits to enter a hospital. I and my brothers and sister might have lost hope—as so many young people today have lost hope—except for the stable, caring, attentive adults in our family, school, congregation, civic and political life who struggled with and for us against the obstacles we faced and provided us positive alternatives and the sense of possibility we needed.

At Spelman College in Atlanta, I found my Daddy and Mama's values about taking responsibility for your own learning and growth reinforced in the daily (except Saturday) chapel service. Daily chapel attendance was compulsory and enforced by the threat of points taken off one's earned grade average as a result of truancy. For all my rebellion then, I remember now far more from the chapel speakers who came to talk to us about life and the purpose of education than from any class. And during my tenure as chairwoman of Spelman's board, I advocated reinstitution of some compulsory assemblies (monthly, not daily!) so our young women would have to hear what we adults think is important.

Many of my mentors and role models, such as Dr. Benjamin Mays, then president of Morehouse College, Whitney Young, dean of the School of Social Work at Atlanta University and later National Urban League head, M. Carl Holman, a professor at Clark College, later head of the National Urban Coalition, Dr. Howard Thurman, dean of the Chapel at Boston University, and Dr. King, all conveyed the same message as they spoke in Sisters Chapel at Spelman: education is for improving the lives of others and for leaving your community and world better than you found it. Other important influences during my Spelman years—Ella Baker, Septima Clark, Howard Zinn, Charles E. Merrill, Jr., and Samuel Dubois Cook—stretched my vision of the future and of one person's ability to help shape it. I'm still trying to live up to their teachings and to the examples of the extraordinary ordinary people whom I had the privilege to serve and learn from after law school during my civil rights sojourn in Mississippi between 1963 and 1968.

Fannie Lou Hamer, Amzie Moore, Winson and Dovie Hudson, Mae Bertha Carter, school desegregation and voting rights pioneers in Mississippi, and Unita Blackwell, who rose from sharecropper to mayor of rural Mayersville, Mississippi—and countless courageous men and women who gave their voices and homes and lives to get the right to vote and to secure for their children a better life than they had—guide and inspire me still. Those largely unknown and usually unlettered people of courage and commitment, along with my parents, remind me each day to keep trying and to let my little light shine, as Mrs. Hamer sang and did through her inspiring life. In a D.C. neighborhood church, I recently saw a banner that reminded me "there is not enough darkness in the world to snuff out the light of even one small candle."

I have always felt extraordinarily blessed to live in the times I have. As a child and as an adult—as a Black woman—I have had to struggle to understand the world around me. Most Americans remember Dr. King as a great leader. I do too. But I also remember him as someone able to admit how often he was afraid and unsure about his next step. But faith prevailed over fear and uncertainty and fatigue and depression. It was his human vulnerability and his ability to rise above it that I most remember. In this, he was not different from many Black adults whose credo has been to make "a way out of no way."

The Children's Defense Fund was conceived in the cauldron of Mississippi's summer project of 1964 and in the Head Start battles of 1965, where both the great need for and limits of local action were apparent. As a private civil rights lawyer, I learned that I could have only limited, albeit important, impact on meeting epidemic family and child needs in that poor state without coherent national policy and investment strategies to complement community empowerment strategies. I also learned that critical civil and political rights would not mean much to a hungry, homeless, illiterate child and family if they lacked the social and economic means to exercise them. And so children—my own and other people's—became the passion of my personal and professional life. For it is they who are God's presence, promise, and hope for humankind.

PART TWO

Passing on the Legacy of Service

I T IS THE RESPONSIBILITY of every adult—especially parents, educators, and religious leaders—to make sure that children hear what we have learned from the lessons of life and to hear over and over that we love them and that they are not alone. Daddy used to say that in school we got our lessons from our teachers first and then got examined on how well we had learned them. In life the consequences often come first and the lessons afterward. In today's era of AIDS and drugs and violence and too-early and unsafe sex, the consequences can be deadly or last a lifetime. So parental communication, guidance, and example are more crucial than ever.

Too many young people—of all colors, and all walks of life—are growing up today unable to handle life in hard places, without hope, without adequate attention, and without steady internal compasses to navigate the morally polluted seas they must face on the journey to adulthood.

As a result, we are on the verge of losing two generations of Black children and youths to drugs, violence, too-early parenthood, poor health and education, unemployment, family disintegration—and to the spiritual and physical poverty that both breeds and is bred by them. Millions of Latino, Native American, and other minority children face similar threats. And millions of white children of all classes, like too many minority children, are drowning in the meaninglessness of a culture that rewards greed and guile and tells them life is about getting rather than giving.

I believe that we have lost our sense of what is important as a people in a world that is reinventing itself at an unprecedented pace both technologically and politically. My generation learned that to accomplish anything, we had to get off the dime. Our children today must learn to get off the paradigm, over and over, and to be flexible, quick, and smart about it.

Children and young adults—all of us—face dazzling international changes and challenges and extraordinary social and economic upheavals. One single decade's profligacy has changed our nation from a lender to debtor. Our aging population and future work force depend on a shrinking pool of young workers, a majority of whom will be female, minority, or both. Our culturally diverse child and worker population confronts increasing racial and gender intolerance fueled by recession and greed. Our education system is drowning in the wake of the new and flexible skills required in a post-industrial economy. The nurturance of children is at risk as extended families disappear, both parents work, and more children rely on a single parent. A cacophony of cultural messages bombard our children about what they must buy and how they must act to be "with it"— with a nearly deafening silence from too many homes and the too-few moral leaders and positive role models in either our private or public lives. Meanwhile, time and economic pressures mount and are unrelieved by extended family networks or family-friendly private sector and public policies.

Despite these social and cultural tidal waves, I believe there are some enduring spiritual, family, community, and national values and lessons that we need to rediscover in this last decade of this last century in this millennium. I agree with Archibald MacLeish that "there is only one thing more powerful than learning from experience and that is not learning from experience."

As my firstborn son Joshua approached his twenty-first birthday, I thought for many months about what I could give him and his brothers, Jonah and Ezra, as they cross the threshold of adulthood. The next chapter's "Letter to My Sons" and twenty-five of the lessons life has taught me—a spiritual and family dowry—is a response that came to me. Although I have tried to weave the themes of work and family together, I was not able to recreate the symbiosis my parents achieved in simpler, more manageable—though not easy—settings. I was not certain that my children knew as clearly as I knew as a child from my parents what gets me through the day and picks me up when I am down.

On a 1989 walk in the glorious hills of Bellagio, Italy, overlooking the breathtaking promontory of Lake Como, I became acutely conscious of the strong spiritual anchors, footholds, and compasses my parents left their five children to help guide us over the mountains and through the valleys and deserts of life. When I don't know what to do, which way to go, or feel profoundly inadequate to the task at hand, an echo of my father's frequent off-key humming of the spiritual "There Is a Balm in Gilead" wells up in my heart, reminding me that I don't have to preach like the Apostle Paul or Martin King or Jesse Jackson or meet Harvard or Yale or congressional or White House or society's decreed standards of anything to be a useful messenger or servant in the world. My parents' example and messages keep me grounded when I am tempted to lose sight of what is important amidst mounting demands of work and family and a culture that values things and style and packaging and publicity over substance and vision and service and concrete action.

Like so many parents, I worry that I have been so busy trying to make sure my children have had all the opportunities and "things" I didn't have and trying to shield them from all of the problems and barriers I had to face and overcome as a Black child and Black woman, that I may not have shared clearly enough all of the most important things I did have growing up: family and community and spiritual values that helped immunize me, and so many of my generation of Blacks, against the plagues of indifference, defeatism, negativism, selfishness, and hopelessness. Our wills were honed to struggle within ourselves to commit to a life beyond ourselves.

Since my children, like yours, have grown up in a very different world from that of my childhood, with a barrage of competing messages and values, I wanted to share with them in this book what I was taught to remember and what I have learned from reading, meditation, prayer, silence, personal experience, and struggle as I have tried to discern and carry out the tasks assigned me. I want my children to know the values I hold most dear, which do not change no matter the times; that they are in my thoughts and prayers often every day; and that each occupies a very special room in my heart and owns love that is his alone and that can never be occupied by another or taken away by anything he can ever say or do.

This book was written for my sons, but also for parents whose own children, like mine, after a certain age do not welcome parental advice. Occasionally they may listen to another adult, which is why perhaps people should switch children with their neighbors and friends for a while in the teen years! I have feared appearing self-righteous and preachy in my writing; let me hasten to assure you that I am sitting in the front pew struggling every minute to live what I preach. Need I say how miserably and often I fail?

Finally, I wrote this book out of fear and concern for America's future, which is far too important to leave to politicians. The greatest threat to our national security and future comes from no external enemy but from the enemy within—in our loss of strong, moral, family, and community values and support. Parent by parent, youth by youth, voter by voter, professional by professional, congregation by congregation, club by club, community by community, foundation by foundation, corporation by corporation, city by city, county by county, state by

PART THREE

A Letter to My Sons

YOUR SPECIAL
DUAL HERITAGES

I T IS NOT EASY for anybody to grow up, to craft a purposeful role in the world, to develop a positive passion for life, and to discover God's will. If you are of mixed racial and religious heritage, as you are, some small and insecure people whose self-esteem seems to rest on looking down on others whom they perceive as "different" may make growing up and life more challenging. But I hope you will always recognize your rich dual heritage as the special gift and blessing that it is; know deep within yourself who you are; and draw strength and pride from the legacies you have inherited from two peoples—Blacks and Jews—who have survived the worst persecution the world can offer. That in recent history these two peoples were slaves and not enslavers, were segregated and discriminated against and were not segregators and discriminators, is an achievement to be proud rather than ashamed of if you take seriously, as I do, the first principle of every great religion: to treat others as you'd like to be treated. It is the only ethical standard in life you need.

It is utterly exhausting being Black in America—physically, mentally, and emotionally. While many minority groups and women feel similar stress, there is no respite or escape from your badge of color. The daily stress of nonstop racial mindfulness and dealings with too many self-centered people who expect you to be cultural and racial translators and yet feel neither the need nor responsibility to reciprocate—to see or hear you as a human being rather than just as a Black or a woman or a Jew—is wearing. It can be exhausting to be a Black student on a "white" college campus or a Black employee in a "white" institution where some assume you are not as smart as comparable whites. The constant burden to "prove" that you are as smart, as honest, as interesting, as wide-gauging and motivated as any other individual tires you out—as does the need to decide repeatedly whether you'll prove to anybody what they have no right to assume or demand.

I understand the resentment of some young Blacks who have decided "who needs it?" and are opting for Black colleges where their "personness" is not under constant assault and testing. They are freed (for a short while) from having to decide whether to ignore, think about, or challenge the constant daily insensitivities of some whites who expect every Black to be a general expert on everything Black at breakfast, lunch, and dinner when you'd rather discuss art, gossip, or simply listen, or who assume you are less competent than they are because of "affirmative action." Black colleges have done an extraordinary job in preparing many of our young to swim in mainstream society. But there really is no hiding place out there or escape from negative racial attitudes in this era of racial backlash fueled by clever and cynical political and media manipulation. So you have to be ready to meet those attitudes and change them.

Affirmative action does not and should not mean that unqualified people get an advantage. Everybody has to be able to do the work in school or on the job to succeed. Nobody should use affirmative action as a favor, a crutch, or as an excuse not to be prepared or not to do a first-rate job—or to stigmatize.

White Anglo-Saxon males never have felt inferior as a result of their centuries of "affirmative action" and quotas (which are *not* the same) in jobs from which Jews, racial minorities, and women were excluded and too often still are. So while you and your brothers must and can make it on the basis of your individual ability, motivation, and disciplined hard work, do not feel defensive about the judgments of some that affirmative action somehow taints a whole race or you as individuals. Just work as hard as you can to perform up to your ability. You are the person you must compare yourself to. Have your own high standards for performance and conduct, not mine or your Dad's or your employers' or your peers'.

There are no easy answers to the continuing dilemmas of race in America. You must grapple with them like those who have gone before you: DuBois in *The Souls of Black Folk* and James Weldon Johnson and Countee Cullen and Paul Laurence Dunbar and Ralph Ellison and Maya Angelou and James Baldwin and Toni Morrison and Alice Walker and countless Black bards and writers who speak to this extra Black burden. The bottom line, however, is to believe in yourself and not let anybody—of any color—limit or define you solely by race or undermine your acceptance and love inside yourself for who you are. Race and gender are givens of

God, which neither you nor anyone else chose or earned at birth. Your race is a fact. Being racist and sexist are a state of mind and a choice.

Dr. King, James Baldwin, and Malcolm X all reminded us that "whiteness is a state of mind" and that the struggle for racial justice is a struggle of conscience and not of race. As such, it is not just a minority responsibility. (And who created the problem?) Nor can minorities be justified in fueling racial divisions any more than those who mistreated them, however understandable the temptation may be. George Washington Carver once warned against letting any man drag you so low as to make you hate him.

Gandhi advised: "Let our first act every morning be the following resolve: 'I shall not fear anyone on earth. I shall fear only god. I shall bear ill-will towards no one. I shall not submit to injustice from anyone.'" No one, Eleanor Roosevelt said, can make you feel inferior without your consent. *Never* give it. Respect other people only on the basis of their individual character and personal efforts, struggles, and achievements. Never defer to another on the basis of his or her race, religion, gender, class, fame, wealth, or position. Whites did not create Blacks. Men did not create women nor Christians Jews. What then gives any human being the presumption to judge, diminish, or exclude another or expect deference solely on such bases? It does not take character, intellect, or talent to inherit a million dollars or to be born white or male. Why should more admiration be given to those who started life with far more advantages and supports than those with none or few? No person has the right to rain on your dreams. No person has a right to define you on the basis of what you have or what you look like.

Affirm who you are inside regardless of the world's judgments: God's and my very precious children who are loved unconditionally, not for what you do, look like, or own, but simply because you are a gift of a loving God. As parents we often forget to convey this, and I have been as guilty as any, as you well know. Many young people feel, as you have, so much pressure to achieve, to get top grades, high test scores, and good jobs, and to perform well in nonacademic ventures—all of which are important for acquiring the self-discipline needed to improve your life choices. But it is important for us overly perfectionist parents to make clear that you are far more than your SATs, good grades, and trophies. However desirable these achievements are and however proud we are of them, they have no bearing on your intrinsic value or on our love for and acceptance of you as a person. No awards can ever rival the countless little and big joys you have given and continue to give us.

I seek your forgiveness for all the times I talked when I should have listened; got angry when I should have been patient; acted when I should have waited; feared when I should have delighted; scolded when I should have encouraged; criticized when I should have complimented; said no when I should have said yes and said yes when I should have said no. I did not know a whole lot about parenting or how to ask for help. I often tried too hard and wanted and demanded so much, and mistakenly sometimes tried to mold you into my image of what I wanted you to be rather than discovering and nourishing you as you emerged and grew.

Even though I am so proud of each of you in every way, and thank you for making your parents look terrific, I still feel twinges of guilt. As many baseball games as I did attend, I still think about the ones I was late for or missed, when you hit those mighty home runs or pitched a no hitter or caught that impossible ball or got hit by the baseball and had to be rushed to the emergency room. But I was so proud on the latter occasion when Joshua responded to his younger brother Ezra's accident, transported him to the hospital, and calmly summoned us parents.

Most of all, I am sorry for all the times I did not affirm all the wonderful things you are and did that got lost in parental admonitions about things left undone or thought not well enough done. A mixed blessing inherited from my childhood that I still struggle with in my relationship with you, with Dad, with colleagues, and most of all, with myself, is the expectation that things be done well. I admit I still recoil against a society that has so slipped in caring that ordinary human sharing and thoughtfulness appears to warrant a "humanitarian award" and diligent effort seems too often the exception rather than the rule. I loved it when Mother Hale in

Harlem, who takes in AIDS and crack babies, responded in an interview: "I'm not an American hero, I'm a person that loves children." But I regret that with you, my children, I have often tended to point out shortcomings rather than to affirm strengths and extraordinary accomplishments.

Finally, I worry about the effects of my sometimes difficult, even frantic, efforts to balance my responsibilities to you, my own children, and to other people's children with whom you must share schools and streets, the nation and world. Paradoxically, the more I worried about and wanted for you, the more I worried about the children of parents who have so much less. When one of you got a high fever, painful earache, asthma attack, or sports injury, how reassuring it was to be able to pick up the phone and call our pediatrician and take you right in. How enraged I am to think that other parents cannot ease their children's suffering and their own fears because they happened to be born on the wrong side of the tracks, the wrong color, or to lack a job with health insurance or the means to get health care.

Because I am my own boss, I could follow my own rule that you came first in any crunch, and that I would always stay home if you were sick if your Dad couldn't. There were nonetheless times of agonizing choices. But I am ever mindful that I had and have real choices. I could leave my office and skip a meeting to care for you or to meet with your teacher without fear of loss of job. Besides, I had two partners in raising you: your Dad and

Miz Amie, our live-in "grandmother" for thirteen years, who treated you as her own. Still I felt uneasy leaving and not being home on a few occasions when you were ill, even with these equally good caregivers. These queasy feelings have goaded me to battle senseless and insensitive national and corporate policies and priorities that don't enable most parents to leave work to care for sick family members, unlike so many other industrialized nations. I cannot imagine leaving you home alone sick and being able to focus on my work.

While I have attended most school parent meetings, I've done so often tired or stressed. When you were in three different schools and I was trying to keep up with your activities and teachers and go off to PTA meetings at night and to attend important school meetings, assemblies, or teacher conferences during the day, I'd imagine what it's like for millions of poor or single parents in unsafe neighborhoods trying to stay actively involved in their children's school without a car or a babysitter. I've tried to cook my share of brownies and chocolate chip cookies, but I've also tried, like my parents, to face the reality that there are problems in the world that all of us must try to address in our own ways. As a parent I believe that protecting you—my own children—does not end in our kitchen or at our front door or with narrow attention just to your personal needs.

As you have grown toward adulthood, you have become increasingly aware that your educationally and financially privileged lives are not typical of other children in this world, nation, or even our own city. We live in one of the wealthiest neighborhoods of Washington, D.C., while thousands of children ten minutes away are living in a war zone that imprisons them in fear and near–Third World poverty. First World privilege and Third World deprivation and rage are struggling to co-exist not only in our nation's capital but all over an America that has the capacity but not the moral commitment and political will to protect all its young.

You must walk the streets with other people's children and attend schools with other people's children. You breathe polluted air and eat polluted food like millions of other children and are threatened by pesticides and chemicals and toxic wastes and a depleted ozone layer like everybody's children. Drunken drivers and crack addicts on the streets are a menace to every American child. So are violent television shows and movies and incessant advertising and cultural signals that hawk profligate consumption and excessive violence and tell you slick is real. It is too easy and unrealistic to say these forces can be tuned out just by individual parental vigilance.

So as a parent I wanted to make sure you had all your physical needs met and a lot of love. But as a parent I could not ignore other people's children or pain that spills over to public space and threatens the safety and quality of life and pocketbook and future of every American. I also wanted to make sure I left you a community and future more safe and hopeful than the one I inherited, and an example of one person trying to make a difference.

Just as parents help shape children, children help shape parents, and you have helped me grow. Thank you for being so helpful and so forbearing.

I hope so much that the balance of your childhood memories will be positive and loving. I worry God a lot not to let my shortcomings as a mother limit your growth or weaken your self-esteem. Indeed, I pray that my weaknesses will strengthen you and that my never-ending and always failing struggle to live what I preach will be a goad rather than impediment to your healthy development.

Parents are sometimes frail and troubled, but also strong and resilient human beings—just like you—if we get the nurturing and support all humans need. Most of us try to keep growing just as you do, although we make lots of mistakes all the time. What we owe you, our children, is our best effort to be a person worth emulating and to send through our lives a message to the future we hope you will feel is worth transmitting to your children and grandchildren. I hope I can grow big enough one day to feel I have done that.

You may think I think that I have all the answers, but like so many of my elders whom I seek to follow, I am often filled with uncertainties. There are a whole lot of mornings when I can barely face the work I know I must do and feel discouraged and hopeless about whether America is ever going to finish the business of ensuring racial and economic and gender justice. And then I see cynical and racist politicians on the television screen and I wonder how we have come to this point *again* in America—after all the struggles and progress of the past thirty years. I cannot believe that you, my children, may have to fight all over again the battles I thought were over.

I won't stop fighting as long as those who would turn us back won't stop. I am terrified by the escalating violence in our country and the apathy and ignorance that feed it. But I ask myself if I believe in my vision of America any less than the hatemongers and those who support them do in theirs. And I remember everything I have been given and all the chances each of us in this country has been given to make a difference.

My life is one of the countless lives that attest to the vibrancy of the American Dream under circumstances much harder than today's. The segregated world of my childhood in the 1940s and early 1950s seemed impenetrable. Never could I have envisaged the positive changes I have seen since my youth. But my parents and elders dreamed of them and never lost hope. So neither will I lose hope that America's best self will overcome growing racial and class divisions. President Havel of Czechoslovakia, when he was in prison, described hope as a state of mind, not a state of the world: "Either we have hope within us or we don't: it is a dimension of the soul. . . . Hope in this deep and powerful sense is . . . an ability to work for something because it is good, not just because it stands a chance to succeed. . . . It is also this hope, above all, which gives us the strength to live and continually to try new things, even in conditions that seem as hopeless as ours do here and now."

I therefore hope you find a positive passion in your life that gives meaning. I hope you find a loving partner to share the way. I hope some of the twenty-five lessons, offered with great love and prayers, will help you around and over some of the rocks ahead that I know you will negotiate with confidence and grace.

Please take this letter and the lessons that follow it in the spirit in which they are given—as tokens of how much you mean to me and as the best road maps I can share with you today. You will obviously ignore, revise, or use all or any of them as you see fit. I have every confidence in your ability to make your own choices. I hope some of these bits of your heritage will be worthy of carrying along to your children and to their children's children—as lanterns of love to lighten and enlighten your and their paths. I am so proud of you in every way and love you more than I can ever say.

PART FOUR

Twenty-Five Lessons for Life

LESSON 1: *There is no free lunch. Don't feel entitled to anything you don't sweat and struggle for.* And help our nation understand that it's not entitled to world leadership based on the past or on what we say rather than how well we perform and meet changing world needs. Every African American, Latino, Asian American, and Native American youth needs to remember that he or she never can take anything for granted in America—especially now as racial intolerance resurges all over our land. Some of it, like David Duke's KKK brand of racism or the 1988 Bush campaign's cynical manipulation of Willie Horton, is blatant. But some of it is more subtle, technical, and very polite. Although it may be wrapped up in new euphemisms and better etiquette, as Frederick Douglass warned, it's the same old snake.

Young white people who have been raised to feel entitled to leadership by accident of birth need to be reminded that the world they face is already two-thirds nonwhite and poor and that our nation is every day becoming a mosaic of greater diversity. Of the total growth in the American labor force between 1988 and 2000, only one in eight of these new additions will be white non-Latino males. As our fate becomes more and more intertwined with that of non-English-speaking people of color—in California, Texas, New York, Iraq, Iran, South Africa, and Japan—personal, economic, and world survival will depend on awareness of and respect for other races and cultures.

Each American adult and child must struggle to achieve and not think for a moment that America has got it made. Frederick Douglass reminded all of us that "men may not get all they pay for in this world, but they must certainly pay for all they get."

While a college degree today may get you in the door, it will not get you to the top of the career ladder or keep you there. You have got to work your way up— hard and continuously. So we need to teach our children—by example—not to be lazy, to do their homework, to pay attention to detail, to take care and pride in work, to be reliable, and not to wobble and jerk through life. Each of us must take the initiative to create our opportunities, not waiting around for favors. We must not assume a door is closed but must push on it. We must not assume if it was closed yesterday that it's closed today.

The rhetoric of the 1980s that told us we could have our cake and eat it too was a recipe for national disaster. A people unable or unwilling to share, to juggle difficult, competing demands, and to make hard choices and sacrifices may be incapable of taking courageous action to rebuild family and community and to prepare for the future. Many whites favor racial justice as long as things remain the same. Many voters hate Congress, but love their own member of Congress as long as he or she takes care of their special interests. Many husbands are happier to share their wives' added income than the housework and child care. Many Americans decry the growing gap between the rich and the poor and middle class, are outraged at escalating child suffering, and favor government action as long as somebody else's taxes are raised and somebody else's program is cut.

Are we going to be able to rise above this national adolescence and deal as a mature people with problems we *can* solve with sustained personal, community, private sector, and governmental efforts?

LESSON 2: *Set goals and work quietly and systematically toward them.* We must all try to resist quick-fix, simplistic answers and easy gains, which often disappear just as quickly as they come. Don't feel compelled to talk if you don't have anything to say that matters. It's all right to feel important if it is not at the expense of doing important deeds. But so many of us talk big and act small. T. S. Eliot, in his play *The Cocktail Party,* said that "half the harm that is done in this world is due to people who want to feel important." You can achieve much in life if you don't mind doing the work and giving others the credit. You know what you do and the Lord knows what you do and that's all that matters.

LESSON 3: *Assign yourself.* My Daddy used to ask us whether the teacher had given us any homework. If we said no, he'd say, "Well, assign yourself." Don't wait around for your boss or your co-worker or spouse to direct you to do what you are able to figure out and do for yourself. Don't do just as little as you can to get by.

If someone asks you to do A, and B and C obviously need to be done as well, do them without waiting to be asked or expecting a Nobel prize for doing what is needed. Too often today too many ordinary, thoughtful deeds are treated as extraordinary acts of valor. Democracy is not a spectator sport. Vote. And don't hide behind the excuse that one vote doesn't count. Don't just complain about our political leaders: run for political office, especially school boards. Those with a special commitment to children and families and the needy have a special role to play in public life. But please don't think that your position or your reelection are the only point once you gain office. Children are. Results are. If you see a need, don't ask, "Why doesn't somebody do something?" Ask, "Why don't I do something?" Don't wait around to be told what to do. There is nothing more wearing than people who have to be asked or reminded to do things repeatedly. Hard work, initiative, and persistence are still the nonmagic carpets to success. Let's each commit to help teach the rest of the country how to achieve again by our example.

LESSON 4: *Never work just for money or for power. They won't save your soul or build a decent family or help you sleep at night.* We are the richest nation on earth, yet our incarceration, drug addiction, and child poverty rates are among the highest in the industrialized world. Don't condone or tolerate moral corruption whether it's found in high or low places, whatever its color. It is not okay to push or use drugs even if every person in America is doing it. It is not okay to cheat or lie even if countless corporate or public officials and everybody you know do. Be honest. And demand that those who represent you be honest. Don't confuse legality with morality. Dr. King noted that everything Hitler did in Nazi Germany was legal. Don't give anyone the proxy for your conscience. And don't confuse legality with fairness. The policies that took tens of billions of dollars from the poor and middle class and gave them to the very rich in the 1980s as tax loopholes and capital gains were legal. But they were not just. That 106 employees at Salomon Brothers can make over a million in one year—the equivalent of what 15,000 families who live at half the poverty level in America must survive on each year—is legal. But it's not fair. Somehow we are going to have to develop a concept of *enough* for those at the top and at the bottom so that the necessities of the many are not sacrificed for the luxuries of the few. I do not begrudge billionaires or millionaires their incomes as long as children's basic needs of food and health and shelter and child care and education are met. But something's out of balance when the number of millionaires in the 1980s almost doubled and the number of poor children increased by three million—almost 30 percent—and children and the poor still face a vastly uneven playing field in the budget process compared with the military and the wealthy. Every dollar for domestic and poor children's program spending requires a huge fight, while the military trough seems bottomless, even as Communism is crumbling worldwide and violence and child abuse and neglect and poverty and joblessness are epidemic nationwide. It is time for America to give children and parents the same floor of social security we provided the elderly in 1972. And last don't, like our nation, spend more than every dollar you earn. Save a dime and share a dime.

LESSON 5: *Don't be afraid of taking risks or of being criticized.* An anonymous sage said, "If you don't want to be criticized don't say anything, do anything, or be anything." Don't be afraid of failing. It's the way you learn to do things right. It doesn't matter how many times you fall down. What matters is how many times you get up. And don't wait for everybody else before you to do something. It's always a few people who get things done and keep things going. This country needs more wise and courageous shepherds and fewer sheep.

As a young civil rights lawyer in Mississippi, I remember wanting somehow to provide solace to a beleaguered Dr. King, who was being attacked by friend and foe alike for speaking out against the Vietnam War. I mailed him Theodore Roosevelt's statement: "It's not the critic who counts. Not the man who points out where the strong man stumbled or where the doer of great deeds could have done them better. The credit belongs to the man who is actually in the arena. Whose face is marred by dust and sweat and blood. Who strives valiantly, who errs and comes up short again and again. And who, while daring greatly, spends himself in a worthy cause so that his place may not be among those cold and timid souls who know neither victory nor defeat."

My youthful gesture of encouragement was not needed by a man who answered his critics in *The Trumpet of Conscience* with such clarity of mission and courage: "For those who ask the question, 'Aren't you a civil rights leader?'—and thereby mean to exclude me from the movement for peace—I answer by saying that I have worked too long and hard now against segregated public accommodations to end up segregating my moral concern. Justice is indivisible. It must also be said that it would be rather absurd to work passionately and unrelentingly for integrated schools and not be concerned about the survival of a world in which to be integrated."

LESSON 6: *Take parenting and family life seriously and insist that those you work for and who represent you do.* Our leaders mouth family values they do not practice. As a result, our children lag behind the children of other nations on key child indicators like infant mortality, poverty, and family supports. Seventy nations provide medical care and financial assistance to all pregnant women; we aren't one of them. Seventeen industrialized nations have paid maternity leave programs; we are not one of them. In 1990 our president vetoed and the business community opposed—and continues to oppose—

an unpaid parental leave bill to enable parents to stay home when a child is born, adopted, or sick. More than half of mothers of infants are in the labor force. Yet too many men in Congress and in the White House still are bickering about whether we can afford funding guarantees for Head Start to get all eligible poor children ready for school. Too many balk at adequately funding the newly enacted comprehensive child care bill to provide safe, affordable, quality child care for millions of parents who must work outside the home, and they balk at providing adequate and refundable tax credits, health insurance, and income supports for working families when one parent remains at home. Since too many men in power still just don't get how hard it is to juggle work and family burdens, it is time for the struggling, beleaguered mothers—and supportive fathers—of this nation to tell our leaders to get with it and stop the political hypocrisy so that all parents can have a real choice about whether to remain at home or work outside the home without worrying about the safety and well being of their children.

Men should not father children until they are able and willing to be responsible for the consequences of childbearing. And all men—young and old, rich, middle and lower income, and poor—should be held accountable for supporting their children. It is shameful that only a small percentage of divorced and unmarried fathers provide any regular child support.

I agree with Mrs. Bush's sentiments expressed at Wellesley College's commencement in 1990 about the importance of family. I too would rather be remembered well by my children for shared times together than for any thousand awards or career successes. But I also understand that millions of mothers and fathers cannot do what she and I can do—choose whether and when to work outside the home because we have enough family income through our husbands or can earn enough ourselves to afford the best child care in our homes. Poor parents and middle-class parents who work outside the home do not need more guilt trips. They need help and real choices. The nation has a responsibility to the millions of low- and middle-income parents, especially mothers, who now can choose neither to stay at home without worrying about providing health care, food, and housing for their children nor to get a job that pays adequate wages and find and afford good child care.

Sixty-three nations worldwide provide a family allowance to workers and their children; America does not. One reason is that too many of us believe the poor have oodles of babies just to get on welfare and that many parents will not spend the money they are given on their children. But nearly two-thirds of poor families with children have only one or two children—no more than the rest of us—and they struggle to make ends meet in ways most Americans could not manage. A typical poor family with children pays 70 percent of its income for housing. We think all poor people are inner-city Black people. But the majority of the poor work; most do not live in inner cities. Most important, their children

This is the marriage model of my childhood. Both my parents cared for children inside and outside the home and did whatever needed to be done in the house and in the community. My father wanted a neater house than my mother so as many chores were done with him as with my mother. (Daddy never could braid hair very well, though, and sent me across the street to my neighbor's house to get this done whenever my mother was in New York visiting her parents.) Daddy was the preacher and teacher and Mama the church organizer and fundraiser. My mother took me along as she raised money for the church and organized and met with her Mother's Club, which planned many church events. Whether cleaning up the house or the church, helping prepare the Sunday bulletin, visiting the sick and the poor, or overseeing homework around the dining room table at night, my parents did not tell us what to do— they did it with us. When Daddy's sister, Aunt Ira, got widowed, she and three of her children came to live in Bennettsville. Daddy and Mama treated those children like their own. After Daddy died and his Aunt Cora became old and ill, my mother brought her to Bennettsville and cared for her until she died. My cousin Artisse wrote me a long letter recently, recounting how Daddy, whom they called Uncle Jerome, constantly counseled them to "be somebody." Artisse recalled how my Daddy and Mama "helped others by giving them work to help themselves" and that "there was no difference in the treatment of persons in their house." She remembered that one of the children who was recovering from TB was included in everything.

We children always knew Daddy as the strong and out-front leader, although Mama's entrepreneurial spirit was never far beneath the surface. She always had a dime squirreled away for crisis, ran her own dairy for a while, and was never without an idea about how to manage in a crunch. Daddy could not have kept the church solvent without her fundraising. When she had to make ends meet and get me and my brother Julian through college after Daddy died, she continued the old folks home and her church fundraising and organist roles as well as taking in twelve foster children. Like Mama, I have always wanted to earn my own dime.

My childhood made me assume that the men of my generation, like my Daddy and my brothers, knew that they were supposed to help and knew how to help. But too many men didn't and still don't. I hope your generation will break this cycle, and I'm pleased by the evidence I see that this may be so. Please talk with your wife about work and family responsibilities regularly and adjust with the changing circumstances and needs of your partner. Try to put yourself in your wife's place and encourage her to do the same with you. Talk often about what you feel—constructively—and do not let anger and rage build up. Your father and I, like so many couples of my generation, would have avoided a great deal of stress if we had known better from the outset how to discuss and share the changing work-family demands and expectations within our marriage. But we have grown and learned from each other. Superwoman simply died of exhaustion. Marriage partners must give and then give more if family bonds are not to be strained and snapped by stress and children's need for consistent nurturance is to be met. And employers must develop policies such as parental leave, flex time, and child care so that parental roles are not undermined.

LESSON 8: *Forming families is serious business*. It requires a measure of thoughtful planning, economic stability, and commitment, particularly with the downward spiral of wages and job opportunities for young families of all races and with the rising costs of good child care and housing, which often require more than one employed parent. An upper-middle-class friend recently observed that her daughter and her husband and grandchildren would be homeless if she did not have the good fortune of owning a second house, which they inhabit. Middle-class parents who used to cry when their children left home to go off to college are now crying because they are coming back home after college or graduate school or a divorce because they can't afford a house or otherwise make ends meet.

Parenting is not only a big economic commitment—the cost of raising a child to age eighteen is more than $114,000, not including savings for college and ignoring future inflation—it is also an enormous emotional and personal commitment. I lost my father at fourteen and my mother at forty-five. I still feel both their losses deeply. Nobody told me how hard it is not to be somebody's child—to be an orphan—even as an adult. The personal and national consequences of hundreds of thousands of runaway and throwaway children, boarder babies, and of children shunted about in out-of-home care, as well as the legacy of countless parents of privilege who have emotionally abandoned their children for money, personal pleasure, or work—and of those parents who are stressed daily beyond the limits of survival by joblessness, homelessness, and other family tragedy and isolation—is a terrible story just unfolding. How many children are turning to gangs and cults and drugs and too-early sex to find what they cannot find at home?

All three of you—my very much wanted, and planned, children—were born after I was thirty. And I thank you very much for helping me learn to parent! I'm still working at it. Although your father and I had more help than most young families, we could have used even more. I cannot imagine how so many teen and single mothers or poor mothers cope without the support our family has been blessed with. Even with all the help I had and have as a parent, I am still hanging by my fingernails many days, trying to balance my office and family responsibilities. That's why I feel every effort must be made to prevent premature sexual activity and the nearly one million teen pregnancies in our nation each year. The majority of these pregnancies are among white teens, although Blacks are disproportionately affected.

LESSON 9: *Be honest*. Struggle to live what you say and preach. Call things by their right names. Be moral examples for your children. If you as parents cut corners, your children will too. If you lie, they will too. If you spend all your money on yourselves and tithe no portion of it for charities, colleges, churches, synagogues, and civic causes, your children won't either. And if parents snicker at racial and gender jokes, another generation will pass on the poison adults still have not had the courage to snuff out. Teach your children good manners. "Please" and "thank you" are two of the most important words in the English language. Being considerate of others will take you and them further in life than any college or professional degree.

I hope you will help strengthen the American tradition of family by stressing family rituals: prayers if you are religious, and if not, regular family meals and gatherings. All children need constructive alternatives to the streets and violence, to drugs—including alcohol, killer tobacco, and too-early sex as antidotes to boredom and drift. But parents alone are not responsible for the perversions of family and community values today. It's harder to parent today and to control your children's values when public figures and advertisers equate drinking with fun and relaxation and glamour; when many television programs and movies seed and feed an apparently insatiable American appetite for gratuitous violence; and when unmarried parents dot the covers of best-selling magazines. Telling our children to "just say no" is hypocritical and useless while parent and other adult role models send cultural messages and provide examples that "say yes." And if millions of parents are children themselves, are single, and have to work because they don't want the stigma of welfare, or are so poor that they have to worry first about food and shelter, where are the children to find the buffers and countersignals they need? Where are the religious leaders? Where are the grandparents? Where are the extended parents? Where are our children supposed to see and grasp a sense of the future?

It is long past time for us to join together as an entire nation and in every community to establish an ethic of service and achievement and to help support strong families for all our children—poor, middle class, and rich— so that the lure of addiction to things and drugs and easy sex and senseless violence will wane. As Ulysses neared the island of the Sirens, he had himself strapped to the ship's mast after his sailors stuffed their ears with wax to try to avoid the enticement of the Sirens' music. Orpheus was able to ignore the Sirens' songs by playing his own beautiful music that rendered them unalluring. Over $1.4 billion per year of new juvenile detention facilities and prisons are not stanching the growing alienation and violence among our young, who lack a purposeful, joyful song to sing in life—a song that is learned first in the home and reinforced in school and in other community institutions and by the religious and political values and climate in our society. Too many of our children are adrift today because too many parents, other adults, and political and business leaders give no thought to teaching by positive example. James Baldwin was right when he said our children do not follow our words but our actions.

LESSON 10: *Remember and help America remember that the fellowship of human beings is more important than the fellowship of race and class and gender in a democratic society.* Be decent and fair and insist that others be so in your presence. Don't tell, laugh at, or in any way acquiesce to racial, ethnic, religious, or gender jokes or to any practices intended to demean rather than enhance another human being. Walk away from them. Stare them down. Make them unacceptable in your homes, religious congregations, and clubs. Through daily moral consciousness counter the proliferating voices of racial and ethnic and religious division that are gaining respectability over the land, including on college campuses. Let's face up to rather than ignore our growing racial problems, which are America's historical and future Achilles' heel.

How many potential Colin Powells, Bill Cosbys, Alice Walkers, Condoleezza Rices, Sally Rides, Gloria Steinems, Barbara McClintocks, Wilma Mankillers, Daniel Inouyes, Henry Cisneroses, and Cesar Chavezes will our nation waste before it wakes up and recognizes that its ability to compete and lead in the new century is as inextricably intertwined with its poor and nonwhite children as with its white and privileged ones, with its girls as well as its boys? Every one of our shrinking pool of children should be seen as a blessing rather than a burden: as potential leaders and workers rather than as problems. We tend to get what we expect and seek.

Let's not spend time pining and denying blame rather than healing our divisions. Rabbi Abraham Heschel put it aptly: "We are not all equally guilty but we are all equally responsible" for building a decent and just America.

After 600,000 American deaths in a civil war to preserve the union and to abolish slavery; 3,437 lynchings of Black Americans since reconstruction; and dozens of deaths during the nonviolent civil rights struggles of the 1960s to help our country live up to American ideals of equal justice under the law, every citizen should reject any political candidate in 1992 and in any year who manipulates racial fears for political gain.

I endorse strongly Iowa Republican Representative Jim Leach's call for "a new political ethic" and for candidates to sign a pledge of tolerance and to make a compact with the electorate not to divide society on the basis of race, religion, ethnicity, age, or place of national origin. "For American reality to match American ideals," he said, "public officials have a special responsibility to uplift rather than tear down, to unify rather than divide." So do you and I.

LESSON 11: *Sell the shadow for the substance.* Don't confuse style with substance; don't confuse political charm or rhetoric with decency or sound policy. I have found it wonderful to go to the White House or Congress or to the State House for a chat, but I remind myself at these times that words and schmoozing alone do not meet children's or the nation's needs. Political leadership and different budget priorities do. Speak truth to power. And put your own money and leadership behind rhetoric about concern for families and children in your own homes, classrooms, law firms, medical practices, corporations, or wherever you pursue your career. There's nothing wrong with wanting a BMW or nice clothes. But BMW is not an advanced degree and a designer coat or jacket is not a life goal or worth a life. I was watching one of President Johnson's inaugural balls on television with a Black college president's wife in Mississippi when Mrs. Hamer, that great lady of the Mississippi civil rights movement who lacked a college degree, but certainly not intelligence or clear purpose, came onto the screen. The college president's wife moaned: "Oh my, there's Miz Hamer at the President's ball and she doesn't even have on a long dress." My response was: "That's all right. Mrs. Hamer with no long gown is there and you and I with our long gowns are not." Nobody ever asks what kind of car Ralph Bunche or Reinhold Niebuhr drove or who designed Martin Luther King, Jr.'s, or Dorothy Day's clothes or who built Mary McLeod Bethune's or Lloyd Garrison's house. Don't confuse style with meaning. Get your insides in order and your direction clear first and then worry about your clothes and your wheels. You may need them less.

Just as we must struggle to keep our personal priorities straight, we also must struggle to keep our organizational and public priorities straight. Dr. King once chided a Black fraternity audience which boastfully announced that its membership had spent $500,000 for liquor. He said, "A handful of Negroes . . . spent more money in one week for whiskey than all of the 16 million Negroes spent that whole year for the UNCF and for the NAACP. Now that was a tragedy." If any Black organization is still spending nearly as much on alcohol and entertainment as on supporting Black institutions and Black children, it is an even greater tragedy. And if most white citizens still prefer to spend more on entertainment and luxury items than on child health and nutrition, America is going to miss the boat to the future. Let's be clear: tobacco and alcohol are killing more black and white people than cocaine. It's time for a critical mass of consumers to speak out against and stop the marketing of sickness and death to our children in sports arenas and parks, during TV sports events and other programs, in movies, or anywhere.

LESSON 12: *Never give up.* Never think life is not worth living. I don't care how hard it gets. An old proverb reminds: "When you get to your wit's end, remember that God lives there." Harriet Beecher Stowe wrote that when you get into a "tight place and everything goes against you, till it seems as though you could not hang on a minute longer, never give up then, for that is just the place and time that the tide will turn." Hang in with life. Hang in for what you believe is right even if every other soul is going a different way. Don't give in to cynicism or despair or dismiss as unsolvable the great challenges of peace or nuclear survival, racial division, poverty, and environmental devastation. Sissela Bok, in her *Alva Myrdal: A Life,* quotes the Nobel Peace laureate: "I know only two things for certain. One is that we gain nothing by walking around the difficulties and merely indulging in wishful thinking. The other is that there is always something one can do oneself. In the most modest form, this means: to study, to try to sort out different proposals, and weigh the effect of proposed solutions—even if they are only partial solutions. Otherwise there would be nothing left but to give up. And it is not worthy of human beings to give up. . . . The greatness of being human . . . lies in not giving up, in not accepting one's own limitations." A little saying I picked up in a convent I visit sometimes echoes her feelings: "God never meant to make life easy, he meant to make men (and women) great"—like Alva Myrdal.

LESSON 13: *Be confident that you can make a difference.* Don't get overwhelmed. Sometimes when I get frantic about all I have to do and spin my wheels, I try to recall Carlyle's advice: "Our main business is not to see what lies dimly at a distance, but to do what lies clearly at hand." Try to take each day and each task as they come, breaking them down into manageable pieces for action while struggling to see the whole. And don't think you have to "win" immediately or even at all to make a difference.

In *The Irony of American History,* Reinhold Niebuhr said: "Nothing that is worth doing can be achieved in our lifetime; therefore we must be saved by hope. Nothing which is true or beautiful or good makes complete sense in any immediate context of history; therefore we must be saved by faith. Nothing we do, however virtuous, can be accomplished alone; therefore we are saved by love. No virtuous act is quite as virtuous from the standpoint of our friend or foe as it is from our standpoint. Therefore we must be saved by the final favor of love which is forgiveness." Remember that sometimes it's important to lose for things that matter and that many fruits of your labor will not become manifest for many, many years.

And do not think that you have to make big waves in order to contribute. My role model, Sojourner Truth, slave woman, could neither read nor write but could not stand slavery and second-class treatment of women. One day during an anti-slavery speech she was heckled by an old man. "Old woman, do you think that your talk about slavery does any good? Why I don't care any more for your talk than I do for the bite of a flea." "Perhaps not, but the Lord willing, I'll keep you scratching," she replied.

A lot of people think they have to be big dogs to make a difference. That's not true. You just need to be a flea for justice bent on building a more decent home life, neighborhood, work place, and America. Enough committed fleas biting strategically can make even the biggest dog uncomfortable and transform even the biggest nation, as we will and must transform America in the 1990s.

Be a flea for justice wherever you are and in whatever career you choose in life and help transform America by biting political and business leaders until they respond.

LESSON 14: *Don't ever stop learning and improving your mind* or you're going to get left behind. The world is changing like a kaleidoscope right before our eyes. College pays and is a fine investment. It doubles your chance of getting a job over a high school graduate. But don't think you can park there or relegate your mind's and soul's growth to what you have learned or will learn at school. Read. Not just what you have to read for class or work, but to learn from the wisdom and joys and mistakes of others. No time is ever wasted if you have a book along as a companion.

My Daddy valued reading almost as much as prayer, service, and work. After my older siblings left home, he used to make me sit with him each evening before the fireplace in his bedroom to read for a spell. When I was twelve or thirteen, I tried to trick him once by slipping a forbidden *True Confessions* magazine into the *Life* magazine I pretended to read. He caught me and asked me to read it aloud and comment on its value! I've not had any appetite for *True Confessions* since!

We always had more books and magazines than clothes or luxuries in our home: the complete works of Mark Twain, Carl Sandburg's multiple volumes on Abraham Lincoln, books about and by great world and American Black leaders. Names like Gandhi, Harry Emerson Fosdick, Paul Tillich, Reinhold Niebuhr, Benjamin Mays, Howard Thurman, W. E. B. DuBois, James Weldon Johnson, and Langston Hughes were etched into my consciousness from very early childhood. Pictures of great doers (of all colors) and clippings of great events (current and historical) dotted the walls of Daddy's study where he withdrew each day to read and think—a father's bulletin board on the big world beyond our small rural town. All of this was, I think, the reason why I always thought the whole world was mine to explore and why I still resist anyone's efforts to relegate only a part of it to me—or to any child.

Daddy stretched us continuously and instilled a sense that all was possible with faith and hard work. He believed in learning by example, exposure, and osmosis. Any time a great Black man or woman came within 200 miles of our hometown, we children were piled in the car to hear them—singers Roland Hayes, Dorothy Maynor, Marian Anderson, and poet Langston Hughes. Great Black preachers and educators were special favorites. I remember sitting on (sometimes snoozing on) very hard seats as a young child through three- or four-hour lectures by Mordecai Johnson, former president of Howard University, who came on a number of occasions to the Columbia, South Carolina, auditorium about a hundred miles away from our hometown—and I still feel stiff. I can hear, as if yesterday, Mary McLeod Bethune's stories over dinner at Benedict College (also in Columbia)—stories of how she challenged segregation, of going into segregated white stores and demanding to try on hats, brushing aside shocked white clerks' refusals with: "Do you know who I am? I am Mary McLeod Bethune!" It was from her mouth that as a child I first heard the phrase "the blacker the berry, the sweeter the juice." She basked with pride in her blackness and helped excise from my young Black female psyche the notion that racial and gender barriers should ever be more than momentary impediments to be knocked down by will and unwavering purpose.

Just as my parents and extended parents imbedded in us children a sense of possibility that transcended the artificial boundaries of our segregated existence, all of today's parents and community leaders must try to give the young bulletins of the great world, through books and great people, so that all children are provided a sense of life that transcends the artificial boundaries of race, gender, class, and things.

LESSON 15: *Don't be afraid of hard work or of teaching your children to work.* Work is dignity and caring and the foundation for a life with meaning. For all her great accomplishments, Mary McLeod Bethune never forgot the importance of practical work. When asked by a train conductor, "Auntie, do you know how to cook good biscuits?" she responded, "Sir, I am an advisor to presidents, the founder of an accredited four-year college, a nationally known leader of women, and founder of the National Council of Negro Women. And yes, I also cook good biscuits."

According to Taylor Branch, in *Parting the Waters,* Vernon Johns, a great Black preacher and one of Dr. King's predecessors at Dexter Avenue Baptist Church in Montgomery, "excoriated Dexter members for their attachment to status and prestige above work ... and preached and scolded and cajoled his congregation about the importance of practical work. . . . He accused them of persisting in the white man's view of slavery— that labor was demeaning—when Negroes should know that it was oppression, not labor, that demeaned them. On the contrary, the desire to avoid labor had enticed whites into the corruption of slavery."

Too many today are embracing an obsession with work to ensure their ability to engage in limitless consumption. But still more children of privilege, of the middle class, and of the poor are growing up without a strong work ethic, and too many are growing up without work at all. An important reason much of my generation stayed out of trouble is that we had to help out at home and in the community and did not have time— or energy—to get into trouble.

LESSON 16: *"Slow Down and Live"* is an African song I sing inside my head when I begin flitting around like a hen with her head wrung off: "Brother slow down and live, brother slow down and live, brother slow down and live, you've got a long way to go. Brothers love one another, brothers love one another, brothers love one another, you've got a long way to go." Since my thoughts and actions and ideas tend to come in spurts and gushes, too often I create tidal waves in my wake, as my family and colleagues can attest. Then St. Francis de Sales reminds me that "rivers that flow gently through the plains carry along larger boats. Rains that fall gently on open fields make them fruitful in grass and grain. Torrents and rivers that spread over the land in great floods ruin the bordering country and are useless for commerce, just as in like manner heavy tempestuous rains ruin the fields and meadows. A job done too . . . hurriedly is never well done." How well I know!

LESSON 17: *Choose your friends carefully.* Stay out of the fast lane, and ignore the crowd. You were born God's original. Try not to become someone's copy. Dr. Benjamin Mays used to tell Morehouse and Spelman College students not to give into peer pressure, saying, "Nobody is wise enough, nobody is good enough, and nobody cares enough for you to turn over to them your future and your destiny." You are the person you must compete with and be accountable for. Rabbi Susya said: "God will not ask me why I was not Moses, He will ask me why I was not Susya."

Dr. J. J. Starks, who served as president of two Black colleges in South Carolina—Morris and Benedict—and who mentored my father, listed six things that destroy students: "Bad company, keeping late hours, gaming as pastime, disregard for values, failure to discriminate between love and lust, and the drink habit." Still sounds pretty good to me.

Find your own niche in life and try to learn to do at least one thing uncommonly well. Follow the need. If you struggle to see and hear and understand and respond to the needs and longings of those all around you—asking how you can serve them rather than how they can serve you—you will not be tempted by fast-lane friends and will never lack for purposeful work doesn't have to be a big work. It just needs to be a ing work.

LESSON 18: *Be a can-do, will-try perso* what you have and not what you don't can do rather than what you cann being paralyzed by can't-doers w punier will. If the Soviet people leader Gorbachev could dism we in America envision an young people under twenty-five voted in the 1988 presidential election. Fewer than 60 percent of women and 52 percent of Blacks used their voting power in 1990. We get the political leaders we deserve. America's children and future are too important to leave to politicians elected by so few. Any American who cannot bother to vote and who thinks that a single vote does not matter is letting America down. In a democratic society—as frustrating as the political process is—if we don't like what our political leaders are doing we must make that clear through our voices and our votes. But we cannot accomplish that staying at home. Together at the polls we can accomplish a new direction for America in 1992 and beyond.

Voting and working in government are only two ways to serve. Diverse opportunities for young people to serve their communities can play a major role in restoring hope and moral example to our nation. Young people need to believe they are needed and adults need to be reminded that our children and youth *all* have something to contribute and are precious resources to be nurtured and cherished. The development of youth service programs across the country reinforces both of these crucial messages, unleashing the creative energies of young people to combat some of our most pressing social problems.

The days of thinking about service as something to occupy the time just of middle-class youths in the suburbs have passed. Indeed, poor and minority youths may profit the most from service activities and give the most in return, *if* we provide the resources in low-income communities to create such opportunities, and if we remove the barriers that sometimes keep them from participating in these programs.

Leadership and service are by no means limited to visible public roles. Be a quiet servant-leader and example in your home, school, workplace, and community. You have a role to exercise either positively or negatively every minute of the day. Have you ever noticed how one example—good or bad—can prompt others to follow? How one illegally parked car can give permission for others to do likewise? How one racial joke can fuel another? How one sour person can dampen a meeting or one complainer sap positive energy? Well, the converse is also true. One or a few positive people can set the tone in an office or congregation or school. Just doing the right and decent thing can set the pace for others to follow in all kinds of settings. America is in urgent need of a band of moral guerrillas who simply decide to do what appears to be right heedless of the immediate consequences. As one anonymous leader said (better than I can): "The world needs more men [and women] who do not have a price at which they can be bought; who do not borrow from integrity to pay for expediency; whose handshake is an ironclad contract; who are not afraid of risk; who are honest in small matters as they are in large ones; whose ambitions are big enough to include others; who know how to win with grace and lose with dignity; who do not believe that shrewdness and cunning and ruthlessness are the three keys to success; who still have friends they made twenty years ago; who are not afraid to go against the grain of popular opinion and do not believe in 'consensus'; who are occasionally wrong and always willing to admit it. In short, the world needs leaders."

America's fate and direction depend on citizen leaders in every nook and cranny of our great nation. Change will come in the 1990s, not from the top down, but from millions of people like you and me raising our voices from the bottom up, telling our religious and political and professional spokespeople what is important to us and holding them accountable. Remember that leaders come in both genders, all sizes, colors, ages, from all geographic areas, and neighborhoods. And they don't all have obvious or special talents. Ved Mehta, in his book *Mohandas Gandhi and His Disciples,* said: "Gandhi was not endowed with any unusual artistic, scholarly, or scientific talents. He never earned a degree or received any special academic honors. He was never a candidate in an election or a holder of public office. Yet when he died, in 1948, at the age of seventy-eight, practically the whole world mourned him."

LESSON 21: *Listen for "the sound of the genuine" within yourself and others.* Meditate and learn to be alone without being lonely. "Small," Einstein said, "is the number of them that see with their own eyes and feel with their own hearts." Try to be one of them.

"There is," Howard Thurman told Spelman College students in 1981, "something in every one of you that waits and listens for the sound of the genuine in yourself." It is "the only true guide you'll ever have. And if you cannot hear it, you will all of your life spend your days on the ends of strings that somebody else pulls."

There are so many noises and pulls and competing demands in our lives that many of us never find out who we are. Learn to be quiet enough to hear the sound of the genuine within yourself so that you can hear it in other people.

It is as necessary as it is hard to practice a regular discipline of silence, solitude, or prayer. I have not fully succeeded but I cannot survive long without my moments. A few minutes every hour, a half hour or hour every day, a day a month, a week a year—in dedicated silence—is a goal to pursue. Even better is the attainment of an internal quiet space within yourself amidst never-ceasing external bedlam. It's tempting to hide behind a too-busy life as an excuse to avoid solitude, and in this I am guiltier than most. But each of us can do what we *really* want to do. St. Francis de Sales recounted how, when St. Catherine of Siena's parents deprived her of time and place to pray and meditate, she simply created a cell within her own heart to dwell in. "The time of business," Brother Lawrence wrote, "does not differ with me from the time of prayer; and in the voice and clatter of my kitchen, while several persons are at the same time calling for different things, I possess

God in as great tranquillity as if I were on my knees at the Blessed Sacrament." I wish I could say this of myself and I heed Gandhi's warning that the world will never be saved if we have to withdraw in order to gain inner peace and balance.

LESSON 22: *You are in charge of your own attitude*—whatever others do or circumstances you face. The only person you can control is yourself. "As human beings," Gandhi said, "our greatness lies not so much in being able to remake the world—that is the myth of the 'Atomic Age'—as in being able to remake ourselves." Worry more about your attitude than your aptitude or lineage. "We who lived in concentration camps," wrote Viktor Frankl, "can remember the men who walked through the huts comforting others, giving away their last piece of bread. They may have been few in numbers, but they offer sufficient proof that everything can be taken from a man but one thing: the last of the human freedoms to [determine one's] attitude in any given set of circumstances—to choose one's own way."

It is not what is done to us that matters, but how we take what is done to us, Archbishop Tutu reminds us. Booker T. Washington did not know his father's name, but it did not keep him from becoming a great man.

You didn't have a choice about the parents you inherited, but you do have a choice about the kind of parent you will be. You may not be able to clean up your neighborhood or street but you can clean up your own house or apartment or room. (Although there are circumstances—trying to parent in rat-infested, peeling, dark, dirty slum apartments—that defy my or anyone else's judgment.) Don't let anything keep you from struggling and seeking to be a decent, striving human being. It is where you are headed not where you are from that will determine where you end up.

After watching the first day of Justice Clarence Thomas's confirmation hearings for the Supreme Court, a friend called me to gripe laughingly about the emotional response of some senators to Thomas's stories of his deprived childhood and how far he had come from the days his family lived in a house with no indoor plumbing. By the senators' standard, my friend observed, half the Black folk of our generation must now be eligible for the Supreme Court, since so many of us who have overcome odds many whites could not imagine grew up, like Thomas, with outhouses!

Don't make excuses. Whether you are poor or rich, don't think that children of privilege don't have to fight for meaning in their lives too. In fact, Booker T. Washington told Tuskegee students that they were blessed compared with some people. "The man or woman who has money, without having had to work for it, who has all the comforts of life, without effort, and who saves his own soul and perhaps the soul of somebody else, such an individual is rare, very rare indeed." Make up your mind that you are not going to allow *anything* to discourage you. Never use physical poverty—or family status and wealth—as an excuse for spiritual poverty. Don't think if you just had money it would solve your problems or empty feelings. Success, Booker T. Washington warned, may injure individuals and institutions (and I'd add countries) more than poverty. Indeed, perhaps America is not hungry enough to listen to and learn from countries with a smaller gross national product whom we perceive as less than peers. The children of the poor have much to teach the children of privilege about the strength that comes from a journey of struggle.

LESSON 23: *Remember your roots, your history, and the forebears' shoulders on which you stand.* And pass these roots on to your children and to other children. Young people who do not know where they come from and the struggle it took to get them where they are now will not know where they are going or what to do for anyone besides themselves if and when they finally get somewhere. All Black children need to feel the rightful pride of a great people that produced Harriet Tubman and Sojourner Truth and Frederick Douglass from slavery, and Benjamin Mays and Martin Luther King and Mrs. Fannie Lou Hamer from segregation—people second to none in helping transform America from a theoretical to a more living democracy.

All children need this pride of heritage and sense of history of their own people and of all the people who make up the mosaic of this great nation. African American and Latino and Asian American and Native American children should know about European history and cultures, and white children should know about the histories and cultures of diverse peoples of color with whom they must share a city, a nation, and a world. I believe in integration. But that does not mean I become someone else or ignore or deny who I am. I learned the Negro National anthem, "Lift Every Voice and Sing," at the same time I learned "The Star Spangled Banner" and "America the Beautiful" and I love them all. I have raised you, my children, to respect other people's children, not to become their children but to become yourselves at your best. I hope others will raise their children to respect you.

LESSON 24: *Be reliable. Be faithful. Finish what you start.* When my sister admonished our aging mother to relinquish some of her many church and community responsibilities, including a home for the aged in which most of the occupants, for whom she was cooking, were younger than she, and also her roles as church organist and chief fundraiser, she replied: "I did not promise the Lord that I was going part of the way. I promised him I was going all the way until he tells me otherwise." America in the 1990s must finish what we started in the Declaration of Independence and Constitution and go all the way until we assure liberty and justice for the millions of children of all races and incomes left behind in our society today despite national leaders who seek to turn us back to the not-so-good old days of race and class and gender divisions.

LESSON 25: *Always remember that you are never alone.* There is nothing you can ever say or do that can take away my or God's love. I cannot improve upon but only repeat some of my Daddy's frequent words on home life and devotion to children. In a 1951 sermon he said: "Parents for today's children must at all cost maintain a home, a center of love for their nurture and security. The pressure of our high-powered civilization is too much for a homeless and loveless child. The growing tragedy of our time is the increasing broken homes. The home—that should be the strongest link in education—is rapidly becoming the weakest ... *Nothing* must separate parents from their duty to their children."

And nothing did separate him or our mother from us—not even death. Whenever my sister and brothers and I get together, we all tell Daddy and Mama stories and laugh as if they are present. I seldom make a big decision or take a big step without wondering what Daddy or Mama would say. And I talk to them at every award ceremony or achievement for myself or you, my children, feeling their invisible but real presence and pride.

My mother and father taught us ways to live and serve and they confirmed Socrates' observation that nothing can harm a good man or woman in this world or the next.

I was privileged to be with both my parents as they prepared to leave and left this life confident that they were not alone. Daddy's last sermon—from the 139th Psalm—told me and the congregation that he was going to "take the wings of the morning and dwell in the ut-termost parts of the sea. Even there shall thy hand lead me, and thy right hand shall hold me fast." He calmly assured my sister Olive during his last few hours not to be afraid: "We are not alone. God is here." And all of his conversation with me in his last conscious moments on the way to the hospital in an ambulance were of the future—about the importance of not letting anything get between me and my education. So as I was awakened from my sleep in the next bed in his hospital room by his final loud breaths and went to summon my mother, sister, and the nurses in the hall to say that Daddy had gone, his peaceful face reassured me and reassures me still. So does my mother's leave-taking as she slipped into a coma still managing to smile and nod as I read on her last night the 103rd and 27th Psalms. "Bless the Lord, O my soul, and all that is within me, bless His holy name." "The Lord is my light and my salvation . . . of whom shall I be afraid." As she sighed her final breaths, my sister Olive and brother Harry and I sang her home.

After my mother's funeral, I rummaged through clippings, letters, magazines, and the scraps of two devoted lifetimes in our home. I was astonished to find how many of the seeds I am still struggling mightily to harvest for children and the poor were planted during my childhood. I found articles on teenage pregnancy, unequal educational opportunity, and Daddy's sermons decrying the breakdown of family and community and the lack of attention to the neediest among us, and insisting that poverty of things is no excuse for poverty of will and spirit. How humbling yet reassuring it was to see that my journey of discovery had both begun and led me back home. How eerie to flip through copies of Daddy's old *Christian Century* magazines piled atop the freezer on the damp inside back porch and to find—folded back to the page and underlined in red by him—a Dwight Eisenhower quotation that I had found decades later in Washington and had made into a Children's Defense Fund poster: "Every gun that is made, every warship launched, every rocket fired signifies a theft from those who hunger and are not fed, those who are cold and not clothed. This world in arms is not spending money alone. It is spending the sweat of its laborers, the genius of its scientists, the hope of its children."

Although you three attended church with me while growing up, we have honored both your father's and my religious traditions in our home. At the beginning of your Bar Mitzvahs in our back yard, my mother on one occasion and my Baptist brothers on two opened by reading the 139th Psalm—affirming not only God's

PART FIVE

If the Child is Safe

A STRUGGLE FOR AMERICA'S CONSCIENCE AND FUTURE

If the child is safe everyone is safe.

— G. Campbell Morgan, "The Children's Playground in the City of God," The Westminster Pulpit (circa 1908)

———

There is no finer investment for any country than putting milk into babies.

— Winston Churchill

The most important work to help our children is done quietly—in our homes and neighborhoods, our parishes and community organizations. No government can love a child and no policy can substitute for a family's care, but clearly families can be helped or hurt in their irreplaceable roles. Government can either support or undermine families as they cope with the moral, social, and economic stresses of caring for children.

There has been an unfortunate, unnecessary, and unreal polarization in discussions of how best to help families. Some emphasize the primary role of moral values and personal responsibility, the sacrifices to be made and the personal behaviors to be avoided, but often ignore or de-emphasize the broader forces which hurt families, e.g., the impact of economics, discrimination, and anti-family policies. Others emphasize the social and economic forces that undermine families and the responsibility of government to meet human needs, but they often neglect the importance of basic values and personal responsibility.

The undeniable fact is that our children's future is shaped both by the values of their parents and the policies of our nation.

— *Putting Children and Families First: A Challenge for our Church, Nation, and World*, National Conference of Catholic Bishops—Pastoral Letter, November 1991

THE 1990s' struggle is for America's conscience and future—a future that is being determined right now in the bodies and minds and spirits of *every* American child—white, African American, Latino, Asian American, Native American, rich, middle class, and poor. Many of the battles for this future will not be as dramatic as Gettysburg or Vietnam or Desert Storm, but they will shape our place in the twenty-first century no less.

Ironically, as Communism is collapsing all around the world, the American Dream is collapsing all around America for millions of children, youths, and families in all racial and income groups. American is pitted against American as economic uncertainty and downturn increase our fears, our business failures, our poverty rates, our racial divisions, and the dangers of political demagoguery.

Family and community values and supports are disintegrating among all races and income groups, reflecting the spiritual as well as economic poverty of our nation. All our children are growing up today in an ethically polluted nation where instant sex without responsibility, instant gratification without effort, instant solutions without sacrifice, getting rather than giving, and hoarding rather than sharing are the too-frequent signals of our mass media, business, and political life.

All our children are threatened by pesticides and toxic wastes and chemicals polluting the air, water, and earth. No parent can shut out completely the pollution of our airwaves and popular culture, which glorify excessive violence, profligate consumption, easy sex and greed, and depict deadly alcohol and tobacco products as fun, glamorous, and macho.

All our children are affected by the absence of enough heroines and heroes in public and daily life, as the standard for success for too many Americans has become personal greed rather than common good, and as it has become enough to just get by rather than do one's best.

All our children are affected by escalating violence fueled by unbridled trafficking in guns and in the drugs that are pervasive in suburb, rural area, and inner city alike.

Young families of all races, on whom we count to raise healthy children for America's future, are in extraordinary trouble. They have suffered since the early 1970s a frightening cycle of plummeting earnings, a near doubling of birth rates among unmarried women, increasing numbers of single-parent families, falling income—the median income of young families with children fell by 26 percent between 1973 and 1989—and skyrocketing poverty rates. Forty percent of all children in families with a household head under thirty are poor. While many middle-class youths and young families see the future as a choice between a house and a child, many undereducated, jobless, poor youths and young adults trapped in inner-city war zones see the future as a choice between prison or death at the hands of gangs and drug dealers.

More and more Americans feel their children are being left behind. But poor children suffer most, and their numbers are growing—841,000 in 1990 alone. They are the small, faceless victims who have no one to speak and fight for them. We were mesmerized by the 1987 death of Lisa Steinberg, a child whose adoption was never completed or abuse detected by our overburdened, inadequate child welfare system. We cheered when Jessica McClure was rescued from an open well shaft in the yard of an unregulated family day care center run by a relative, a danger she should not have come close to in the first place. But when eight-month-old Shamal Jackson died in New York City from low birthweight, poor nutrition, and viral infection—from poverty and homelessness—we didn't hear much about him. During his short life, he slept in shelters with strangers, in hospitals, in welfare hotels, in the welfare office, and in the subways he and his mother rode late at night when there was no place else to go. In the richest nation on earth, he never slept in an apartment or house. Nor have we heard about two-pound "Jason" fighting for his life at Children's Hospital in Washington, D.C., or about thousands of other babies in similar neonatal intensive care wards all over America. At birth—three months before he was due—Jason weighed just over one pound. He lives because tubes connect his lungs and every available vein to the many machines that are needed to feed him and keep him warm and enable him to take his next breath. He has a heart problem and has already suffered seizures because of damage to his nervous system caused by bleeding into his head—damage that, if he lives, will probably be permanent.

What exactly led to Jason's premature birth will never be known. We do know, however, that unless a mother receives early and ongoing prenatal care, conditions that lead to prematurity cannot be detected or treated. A third of our mothers do not receive the care they need because our health care system, unlike that of every other major industrialized nation, does not provide universal basic coverage for mothers and children.

Remember these children behind the statistics. All over America, they are the small human tragedies who will determine the quality and safety and economic security of America's future as much as your and my children will. The decision you and I and our leaders must make is whether we are going to invest in every American child or continue to produce thousands of school dropouts, teen parents, welfare recipients, criminals—many of whom are alienated from a society that turns a deaf ear to the basic human needs and longings of every child.

If recent trends continue, by the end of the century poverty will overtake one in every four children, and the share of children living with single parents will also rise. One in every five births and more than one in three black births in the year 2000 will be to a mother who did not receive cost-effective early prenatal care. One of every five twenty-year-old women will be a mother, and more than four out of five of those young mothers will not be married. And the social security system that all of us count on to support us in our old age will depend on the contributions of fewer children—children we are failing today.

If we do not act immediately to protect America's children and change the misguided national choices that leave too many of them unhealthy, unhoused, ill-fed, and undereducated, during the next four years

1,080,000	American babies will be born at low birth-weight, multiplying their risk of death or disability,
143,619	babies will die before their first birthday,
4,400,000	babies will be born to unmarried women,
2,000,000	babies will be born to teen mothers,
15,856	children 19 or younger will die by firearms,
2,784	children younger than 5 will die by homicide,
9,208	children 19 or younger will commit suicide,
1,620,000	young people ages 16 to 24 will fail to complete high school,
3,780,000	young people will finish high school but not enroll in college,

599,076	children younger than 18 will be arrested for alcohol-related offenses, 359,600 for drug offenses, and 338,292 for violent crimes,
7,911,532	public school students will be suspended, and
3,600,000	infants will be born into poverty.

It is a spiritually impoverished nation that permits infants and children to be the poorest Americans. Over 13 million children in our rich land go without the basic amenities of life—more than the total population of Illinois, Pennsylvania, or Florida. If every citizen in the state of Florida became poor, the president would declare a national disaster. Yet he and Congress have yet to recognize child and family poverty and financial insecurity as the national disaster it is and to attack it with a fraction of the zeal and shared commitment we now apply to digging out after a devastating hurricane or earthquake or fire. We moved more than 1.7 million elderly persons out of poverty in the three years following the 1972 revisions to the Social Security Act that indexed senior citizens' benefits to inflation. Surely we can provide families with children equitable treatment.

It is a morally lost nation that is unable and unwilling to disarm our children and those who kill our children in their school buses, strollers, yards, and schools, in movie theaters, and in McDonald's. Death stalks America's playgrounds and streets without a declaration of war—or even a sustained declaration of concern by our president, Congress, governors, state and local elected officials, and citizens.

Every day, 135,000 children bring a gun to school. In 1987, 415,000 violent crimes occurred in and around schools. Some inner-city children are exposed to violence so routinely that they exhibit post-traumatic stress symptoms similar to those that plague many Vietnam combat veterans. Still, our country is unwilling to take semiautomatic machine guns out of the hands of its citizens. Where are the moral guerrillas and protesters crying out that life at home is as precious as life abroad? Isn't it time for a critical mass of Americans to join our law enforcement agencies and force our political leaders to halt the proliferation of guns? Every day twenty-three teens and young adults are killed by firearms in America.

In response to a distant tyrant, we sent hundreds of thousands of American mothers and fathers, sons and daughters, husbands and wives, sisters and brothers to the Persian Gulf. According to Secretary of State James Baker, the Gulf War was fought to protect our "life style" and standard of living and the rights of the Kuwaiti people. No deficit or recession was allowed to stand in the way. How, then, can we reconcile our failure to engage equally the enemies of poverty and violence and family disintegration within our own nation? When are we going to mobilize and send troops to fight for the "life style" of the 100,000 American children who are homeless each night, to fight for the standard of living of thousands of young families whose earning capacity is eroding and who are struggling to buy homes, pay off college loans, and find and afford child care? Where are the leaders coming to the rescue of millions of poor working- and middle-class families fighting to hold together their fragile households on declining wages and jobs? Why are they not acting to help the one in six families with children headed by a working single mother—29 percent of whom are poor? Isn't it time to tell our leaders to bail out our young families with the same zeal as they bailed out failed thrift and banking institutions to the tune of an estimated $115 billion by 1992?

What do we *really* value as Americans when the president's 1992 budget proposed only $100 million to increase Head Start for *one year* and no addition for child care for working families, but $500 million *each day* for Desert Storm, $90 million *each day* to bail out profligate savings and loan institutions, and hundreds of millions more to give capital gains tax breaks to the rich? Between 1979 and 1989, the average income (adjusted for inflation) of the bottom fifth of families dropped by 6 percent while that of the top fifth surged upward by 17 percent. The poorest fifth of American families with children lost 21 percent of their income.

Why were we able to put hundreds of thousands of troops and support personnel in Saudi Arabia within a few months to fight Saddam Hussein when we are unable to mobilize hundreds of teachers or doctors and nurses and social workers for desperately underserved inner cities and rural areas to fight the tyranny of poverty and ignorance and child neglect and abuse?

Isn't it time for the president and Congress and all of us to redefine our national security and invest as much time and leadership and energy to solving our problems at home as we do to our problems abroad?

It is an ethically confused nation that has allowed truth-telling and moral example to become devalued commodities. Too many of us hold to the philosophy that "government is not the solution to our problems, government is the problem." If government is seen as an illegitimate enterprise, if the public purposes of one's job are not considered a high calling, and if government has no purpose other than its own destruction, the restraints against unethical behavior in both the public and private sectors quickly erode. As a result, for every Michael Deaver and for every Elliot Abrams, from the public sector, there is an Ivan Boesky or a Reverend Jim Bakker in the private sector. If the only principle our society adheres to is economist Adam Smith's "Invisible Hand," it leaves little or no room for the human hand, or the hand of God, whom the prophet Micah said enjoined us "to be fair and just and merciful." There is a hollowness at the core of a society if its members share no common purpose, no mutual goals, no joint vision—nothing to believe in except self-aggrandizement.

Isn't it time for us to hold our political leaders to

their professed beliefs and promises about getting children ready for school and providing them health care and education?

It is a dangerously short-sighted nation that fantasizes absolute self-sufficiency as the only correct way of life. Throughout our history, we have given government help to our people and then have forgotten that fact when it came time to celebrate our people's achievements. Two hundred years ago, Congress granted federal lands to the states to help maintain public schools. In 1862, President Lincoln signed the Morrill Land-Grant Act, granting land for colleges. The first food voucher and energy assistance programs came, not during the New Deal or the War on Poverty, but at the end of the Civil War, when Congress and President Lincoln created the Freedman's Bureau. Federal help for vaccinations, vocational education, and maternal health began, not with Kennedy, Johnson, and Carter, but under Madison, Wilson, and Harding, respectively.

Our parents, grandparents, and great-grandparents benefited from this government help just as we all do today. Only the most blind of economists could doubt that American prosperity, like Japan's, is built on the synergistic relations between government and private initiative. But it is some of the most blind economists, political scientists, and "moral philosophers" who have the ear of many of our leaders or are themselves political leaders. Too many of them suffer from the peculiarly American amnesia or hypocrisy that wants us to think that poor and middle-class families must fend entirely for themselves; that makes us forget how government helps us all, regardless of class; and that makes us believe that the government is simply wasting its billions supporting a wholly dependent, self-perpetuating class of poor people, while doing nothing but taxing the rest of us.

Chrysler and Lee Iacocca didn't do it alone. Defense contractors don't do it alone. Welfare queens can't hold a candle to corporate kings in raiding the public purse. Most wealthy and middle-class families don't do it alone. Yet some begrudge the same security for low- and moderate-income families with children who must grow up healthy, educated, and productive to support our aging population.

The president and Congress and public must take the time and have the courage to make specific choices and not wield an indiscriminate budget ax or hide behind uniform but unjust freezes of current inequalities. They must also take time to distinguish between programs that work (like immunization, preventive health care, and Head Start) and programs that don't (like the B2 stealth bomber). They must apply the same standards of accountability for programs benefiting the rich and poor and middle class alike. They must hold the Pentagon to the same standards of efficiency as social programs. And isn't it time for the president and Congress to invest more in preventing rather than trying to mop up problems after the fact? Isn't it time to reassess national investment priorities in light of changing national and world needs? Does it make sense for our federal government to spend each hour this fiscal year $33.7 million on national defense, $23.6 million on the national debt, $8.7 million on the savings and loan bailout, $2.9 million on education, and $1.8 million on children's health?

Making hard choices and investing in our own people may help restore the confidence of citizens in government. The overarching task of leadership today in every segment of American society is to give our youths, and all Americans, a sense that we can be engaged in enterprises that lend meaning to life, that we can regain control over our families and our national destiny, and that we can make a positive difference individually and collectively in building a decent, safe nation and world.

America cannot afford to waste resources by failing to prevent and curb the national human deficit, which cripples our children's welfare today and costs billions in later remedial and custodial dollars. Every dollar we invest in preventive health care for mothers and children saves more than $3 later. Every dollar put into quality preschool education like Head Start saves $4.75 later. It costs more than twice as much to place a child in foster care as to provide family preservation services. The question is not whether we can afford to invest in every child; it is whether we can afford not to. At a time when future demographic trends guarantee a shortage of young adults who will be workers, soldiers, leaders, and parents, America cannot afford to waste a single child. With unprecedented economic competition from abroad and changing patterns of production at home that demand higher basic educational skills, America cannot wait another minute to do whatever is needed to ensure that today's and tomorrow's workers are well prepared rather than useless and alienated—whatever their color.

We cannot go back and change the last decade's birth rates. But we can prevent and reduce the damages to our children and families and ensure every child a healthy start, a head start, and a fair start right now. In the waning years of the twentieth century, doing what is right for children and doing what is necessary to save our national economic skin have converged.

When the new century dawns with new global economic and military challenges, America will be ready to compete economically and lead morally only if we

1. stop cheating and neglecting our children for selfish, short-sighted, personal, and political gain;

2. stop clinging to our racial past and recognize that America's ideals, future, and fate are as inextricably intertwined with the fate of its poor and nonwhite children as with its privileged and white ones;

3. love our children more than we fear each other and our perceived or real external enemies;

4. acquire the discipline to invest preventively and systematically in all of our children *now* in order to reap a better trained work force and more stable future *tomorrow;*

5. curb the desires of the overprivileged so that the survival needs of the less privileged may be met, and spend less on weapons of death and more on lifelines of constructive development for our citizens;

6. set clear, national, state, city, community, and personal goals for child survival and development, and invest whatever leadership, commitment, time, money, and sustained effort are needed to achieve them;

7. struggle to begin to live our lives in less selfish and more purposeful ways, redefining success by national and individual character and service rather than by national consumption and the superficial barriers of race and class.

The mounting crisis of our children and families is a rebuke to everything America professes to be. While the cost of repairing our crumbling national foundation will be expensive in more ways than one, the cost of not repairing it, or of patching cosmetically, may be fatal.

The place to begin is with ourselves. Care. As you read about or meet some of the children and families in this country who need your help, put yourself in their places as fellow Americans. Imagine you or your spouse being pregnant, and not being able to get enough to eat or see a doctor or know that you have a hospital for delivery. Imagine your child hungry or injured, and you cannot pay for food or find health care. Imagine losing your job and having no income, having your unemployment compensation run out, not being able to pay your note or rent, having no place to sleep with your children, having nothing. Imagine having to stand in a soup line at a church or Salvation Army station after you've worked all your life, or having to sleep in a shelter with strangers and get up and out early each morning, find some place to go with your children, and not know if you can sleep there again that night. If you take the time to imagine this, perhaps you can also take the time to do for them what you would want a fellow citizen to do for you. Volunteer in a homeless shelter or soup kitchen or an afterschool tutoring or mentoring program. Vote. Help to organize your community to speak out for the children who need you. Visit a hospital neonatal intensive care nursery or AIDS and boarder baby ward and spend time rocking and caring for an individual child. Adopt as a pen pal a lonely child who never gets a letter from anyone. Give a youth a summer job. Teach your child tolerance and empathy by your example.

Essential individual service and private charity are not substitutes for public justice, or enough alone to right what's wrong in America. Collective mobilization and political action are also necessary to move our nation forward in the quest for fairness and opportunity for every American.

So pledge to take responsibility not only for your child but for all children or at least for one child who may not be your own. Finally, as you read the prayer below by Ina J. Hughs, include with every "we pray" the promise "I take responsibility for":

We pray for children
   who sneak popsicles before supper,
   who erase holes in math workbooks,
   who can never find their shoes.
And we pray for those
   who stare at photographers from behind barbed wire,
   who can't bound down the street in a new pair of
     sneakers,
   who never "counted potatoes,"
   who are born in places we wouldn't be caught dead,
   who never go to the circus,
   who live in an X-rated world.
We pray for children
   who bring us sticky kisses and fistfuls of dandelions,
   who hug us in a hurry and forget their lunch money.
And we pray for those
   who never get dessert,
   who have no safe blanket to drag behind them,
   who watch their parents watch them die,
   who can't find any bread to steal,
   who don't have any rooms to clean up,
   whose pictures aren't on anybody's dresser,
   whose monsters are real.
We pray for children
   who spend all their allowance before Tuesday,
   who throw tantrums in the grocery store and pick at
     their food,
   who like ghost stories,
   who shove dirty clothes under the bed, and never
     rinse out the tub,
   who get visits from the tooth fairy,
   who don't like to be kissed in front of the carpool,

who squirm in church or temple and scream in the
    phone,
whose tears we sometimes laugh at and
    whose smiles can make us cry.
And we pray for those
    whose nightmares come in the daytime,
    who will eat anything,
    who have never seen a dentist,
    who aren't spoiled by anybody,
    who go to bed hungry and cry themselves to sleep,
    who live and move, but have no being.
We pray for children who want to be carried
    and for those who must,
    for those we never give up on and for those
    who don't get a second chance.
For those we smother . . . and for those who will grab
    the hand of anybody kind enough to offer it.

Please offer your hands to them so that no child is left
behind because we did not act.